Communist

Manifesto

KARL MARX

Communist Manifesto

*With an introduction
by Stefan T. Possony*

 A GATEWAY EDITION

Chicago · HENRY REGNERY COMPANY

Translated by Samuel Moore

Contents

Introduction

THE CONFISCATION
OF HUMAN LIBERTY

THE claim that the *Communist Manifesto* is, with the exception of the Bible, the world's most widely read book hardly can be substantiated. Millions of copies, however, have been printed in all important languages, and the pamphlet's ideas, having been adopted, often unconsciously, by numerous writers, continue to influence political activities in many a country. Though written more than a century ago (1848), the *Manifesto,* even today, remains a historical force.

POLITICAL ORIGINS

Karl Marx wrote the *Manifesto* at the behest of the Communist League, a secret society operating from London. The League's antecedents can be traced to the groups which attempted to carry on with François Noël Babeuf's *conspiracy of the equals,* and to revolutionary outfits associated with the name of Auguste Blanqui, perhaps the greatest rabble-rouser of the 19th century. It originally consisted of German exiles, mostly craftsmen and *not* intellectuals. Gradually, however, it assumed a more international and intellectual character and established contact with other Western European secret societies, as well as with radical groups acting in the open.

Some time during 1846, the League decided to bring together the extreme radical movements of all civilized countries and organize revolution on an international scale. This, it recognized, called for a program acceptable to the revolutionaries of all nations.

Some members of the Communist League had been impressed by the pugnacity of Karl Marx and Friedrich Engels, two young German exiles who were specializing in attacking leftist doctrines for their alleged lack of truly radical content. Especially attractive was their superlative aggressiveness against the more sedate reform ideas of the day which did not postulate the necessary destruction of the social order and thus, because of their lack of élan, passion and violence, were allegedly harmful to the revolutionary cause. Even more important, Marx and Engels claimed that they had unravelled the secret meaning of the historical process and hence possessed the key to the achievement of the revolution.

In the Spring of 1847, the Communist League invited Marx and Engels to develop a program, based on their concept of infallible success. This program was to become the guide for the League's work of revolutionary unification and re-creation of practical revolutionism. Marx and Engels accepted.

A few months later, the Communist League held its first congress in London and decided, or so the story goes, not to engage in conspiracy but to devote all efforts to propaganda. (Many years earlier the partisans of Charles Fourier had made a similar decision.) Shortly afterwards, Moses Hess—who had done more than anyone else to convert Marx and Engels to socialism—submitted a draft program to the Paris group of the Communist League. This was all that was needed to bring Engels, who at the time was having a tender affair with Hess' wife, into action. He prevailed on the group to reject Hess' draft and to charge him, Engels, with the task of elaborating the program. Hastily, he wrote a catechetical 25 questions-and-answers statement, entitled *Foundations of Communism*.

At a second congress of the Communist League in London (November-December 1847), Engels' draft was discussed, together with the ideas of the new revolutionary creed. Marx, who dominated the debate, was asked to take in hand all the available programmatic papers and write a statement whose title, according to a suggestion from Engels, was to be the *Communist Manifesto* or, more accurately, *Manifesto of the Communist Party*. Marx, for whom meeting deadlines never was easy, did not produce as rapidly as had been hoped. On January 26, 1848, he was asked peremptorily to hand in his manuscript by February 1, lest he be subjected to sanctions. Marx complied, and by the end of February 1848 the *Manifesto* was published, in the German language, in England.

THE TIMING OF THE MANIFESTO

One thing worth noting about this timetable is that the Communist League was in such an extreme hurry to publish the *Manifesto*—as witness the pressure on Marx only six or seven weeks after he had been commissioned to write the pamphlet. Another is that the publication of the *Communist Manifesto* coincided with the 1848 revolutions. It was published almost on the day when King Louis Philippe of France was overthrown, less than three weeks before Metternich, the Austrian pillar of conservative government, was forced into exile, and at a moment when the Prussian monarchy was rocked to its very foundations. The *Manifesto*, of course, did not affect these events in the slightest. But one obvious question imposes itself: did the leaders of the Communist League *know* that the revolution was coming and wish the *Manifesto* to be handy for the battles ahead? And, further, assuming that the communist leaders had anticipated revolutionary events: were they just astute observers or were they acting on conspiratorial inside information?

The revolutionary period had begun with an uprising in Sicily (January 12, 1848). The dunning dispatch was sent to Marx two weeks afterwards. The French revolution had been predicted by Alexis de Tocqueville in a parliamentary speech on January 27, 1848. Engels in the *Foundations of Communism* had spoken of an imminent revolution in England. Marx, in the *Manifesto*, had made it clear that he was anticipating a revolution in Germany. Indeed, the political analysts of the period were prophesying revolutionary outbreaks for practically all countries. Europe was in the throes of an economic depression which the then governments were quite incapable of handling. It is therefore permissible to assume that the Communist League, in consonance with the *Zeitgeist*, simply was expecting early unrest and that its pressure on Marx was dictated by a good political sense of appropriate timing. For that matter, many other political parties at the time were busy writing programmatic manifestoes.

Still, the events of 1848 present a riddle to those who are reluctant to believe that revolutions (as distinguished from riots) occur spontaneously, let alone that many revolutions should occur spontaneously *and* simultaneously in different countries, with a presumed urge to imitate as the only connecting link. There are enough data to show that secret societies were very active before and during the revolutionary period, and that they maintained close international contacts. Rarely if ever did a secret society act alone, and it is unlikely that the League did. Engels himself has provided us with some scanty information on this point.

Was there a "conspiracy behind the conspiracy"? Secret wirepullers undoubtedly were at work, but they were not necessarily intent on promoting revolutionary objectives. For example, we know that the Tsar maintained at Paris an office that was in charge of what nowadays is called "political warfare." We know, too, that he had a hearty dislike for Louis Philippe. And we know finally, that the *Deutsche Bruesseler Zeitung*, Marx's literary outlet during 1847, was published by Adalbert von Bornstedt, an erstwhile agent of the Austrian and Prussian governments. Marx allegedly did not believe in Bornstedt's dishonesty. Franz Mehring, Marx's official biographer, explains that since no other channel of communication was open to him, Marx acted wisely in using the *Deutsche Bruesseler Zeitung*. Possibly so; but what exactly were the circumstances which activated the Communist League and which induced the London communists to invite Marx to be their spokesman? Where did the money come from? Was the League following instructions from a hidden source? Was this source a super-secret promoter of revolution? Or was it perhaps a government aiming to revise the political map of Europe?

Probably it was neither, but on the basis of presently available documentation, it is not possible to congeal these uncertainties into a true historical inquiry. We must understand that our information about the organizational and political origins of the *Communist Manifesto* is disappointingly incomplete. Our best and practically only source on the Communist League and its relations with other revolutionary groups is a short report by Engels. It can be shown that, in some particulars, this report is not fully accurate. It is not even known whether *all* the documents available in the *Nachlass* of Marx and Engels have been published.

The Origin of Marx's Ideas

We know, then, very little of the innermost organizational history of the *Communist*

Manifesto. But we do possess all the necessary information about its intellectual antecedents. The *Manifesto* can be described as a summation of all the radical ideas elaborated during the century preceding its publication, with special emphasis on those concepts which would prove most useful as revolutionary incentives. In this sense the *Manifesto* is not unlike the "platform" of a typical contemporary political party. Its authors were making a *synthesis* and felt entitled to draw freely on many sources. Were they not the ghost-writers of a revolutionary clearing house, allegedly representing the "interest of the movement as a whole"—rather than individual authors? They did not, we must note, put their names on the title page. Only from 1872 onward when the *Manifesto* was pulled out from oblivion were Marx and Engels acknowledging authorship by signature. At that time it would have been intellectually honest to admit that the *Manifesto* was more a synthetic than an original work.

To give a few examples of the kind of "borrowing" from other writers that is to be found in the *Manifesto*:

1. The theory that society can be divided

into two classes, the oppressed and the oppressors, and that these two classes constantly have been struggling against each other, had been expressed in 1780 by Gaetano Filangieri, a Neapolitan nobleman and social scientist. It appears also in Helvetius, Marat, Babeuf and, after 1802, in the writings of Saint-Simon and his school. The idea had been developed by Auguste Mignet (1824) and Augustin Thierry (1825 and repeatedly thereafter), by François Guizot (during the 1820's),* Victor Considérant (1843), Benjamin Disraeli (1845), and Alexis de Tocqueville (1847 and January, 1848). The list could be extended, but we content ourselves with pointing out that already by 1844 Feargus O'Connor, the Chartist leader, was using the term "class struggle" as though it were in common usage.

2. The concept of "exploitation" of man by

---

* Guizot was the French prime minister who was attacked in the opening paragraph of the *Manifesto* and who incidentally would have put down the revolution of February, 1848, had not King Louis Philippe been oblivious of the rules of violent class war and objected to the use of force.

man had been defined by Saint-Simon and been enlarged upon by his students Saint-Amand Bazard and Prosper Enfantin; the latter, incidentally, is the originator of the thought that any income not derived from manual labor is exploitation. J. P. Proudhon also had used the concept of exploitation as one of his key arguments. The theory of crises and their revolutionary significance had been expounded by Simonde de Sismondi in 1827. It was repeated often by Considérant and many other writers.

3. The undeniable misery of the working classes, far from having been discovered by Marx and Engels, was the foremost topic of contemporary politics. In 1840 the French Académie des Sciences Morales et Politiques (which had been reactivated by Guizot) had issued a call for research on the subject of poverty. In reply, Eugene Buret had published a book on the French and British working classes, and it was this book which, shortly after its publication, had influenced Engels to write a similar treatise on the British proletariat (1845)—a subject about which he knew a great deal from his personal experiences as an *entrepreneur*. Even conserva-

tives, like the Prince of Monaco (1839) and Prince Louis Napoleon Bonaparte himself (1848) had discussed this burning problem. Eugene Sue had described "pauperism" in vivid colors in his literary works. In England, too, poverty was the most pressing political and social problem. Thomas Carlyle and Charles Dickens had done much to make the public realize that the conditions of manual laborers were intolerable. Benjamin Disraeli had taken, and would continue to take, literary and political interest in an all-out fight against poverty. Incidentally, English local self-government and the British educational system are partly the result of the administration of the "poor laws" of the time. Remember, too, that these were the days of the Irish famine.

4. The key argument of Marx, namely, that the economic situation of the laboring classes would deteriorate catastrophically as capitalism was progressing, not only proved erroneous, but also appears to be the least original of his contentions. Robert Michels has shown that this *Verelendungstheorie* was formulated first by Antonio Genovesi (1756), and later by Giammaria Ortes (1774), whose writings

were well known to Marx. During the 19th century the concept that the rich would grow richer and the poor poorer was expressed by practically all radical writers, including Louis Blanc, Proudhon, Fourier, Considérant, by many liberal conservatives like Adolphe Blanqui, by historians like Jules Michelet, by reform economists like Sismondi, and by classical economists like David Ricardo.

5. The concept that the coming of social-ism would be the result of the "natural" and inexorable development of capitalism toward ever increasing impoverishment, and that the course of history is predetermined as though it were ruled by natural laws, was taken over from Condorcet, Saint-Simon and Auguste Comte. This idea led to Marx's claim that against ever "utopian" or impractical schemes he was setting forth "scientific socialism": instead of arguing about what *ought* to be, Marx affirmed, socialism must concern itself with what *will* be. The future cannot be created. It only can be foreseen, and Marx foresaw—socialism. But again, the term "sci-entific socialism" was borrowed from Prou-dhon, while the thought was strictly within the spirit of Saint-Simon and Hegel.

6. The belief in the creative role of violence (which, of course, has a long history among military writers) had originated among radical thinkers with Mably, Robespierre, Carrier and Babeuf. Through Buonarotti and Auguste Blanqui, it had come down to Marx. The notorious assertion that the "working man has no country" had been expressed, critically, by the English writer Sir Edward Bulwer-Lytton in 1833. And the *Manifesto's* most powerful slogan, "working men of all countries, unite!", seems to have been phrased by Karl Schapper, a leader of the League.

We could continue indefinitely tracing the origins of the various Marxian ideas.* In the end we probably would not disagree too sharply with Werner Sombart's observation that there is not one single new idea in the

* The authors who have traced the history of socialist thought include Thomas G. Masaryk, Antonio Labriola, Charles Andler, Mikhail A. Tugan Baranovski, Georg Adler, Anton Menger, Robert Michels, Werner Sombart, Auguste Cornu, Karl Loewith, Alexander Gray, F. A. Hayek and Eric Voegelin.

Communist Manifesto.* The *Manifesto* is, in fact, an extract from the thoughts of Helvetius, Rousseau, Morelly, Pierre Leroux, Proudhon, Bazard, Enfantin, Buret, Cabet, Dézamy and Considérant on the French side, and from those of Hegel, Heine, Boerne, Gutzkow, Froebel, Feuerbach, Bruno Bauer, Hess and Weitling on the German side. Marx is as little the originator of socialism and communism as the chairman of General Motors Corporation is the inventor of the automobile.

Engels Accredits Marx with Three Original Ideas

In his introduction to the 1888 edition of the *Manifesto* (reproduced in the present edition), Engels gave Marx credit for just three original ideas.

Marx's first alleged contribution was that the history of mankind has been a history

---

* After listing some of Marx's inspirations, it may be pertinent to mention one book which Marx did *not* read: de Tocqueville's *Democracy in America*. The grandiose project of world revolution was based on less than complete factual information.

of class struggles—a senseless exaggeration (although it is true that at all times various human groups have struggled with each other). We have seen that the idea is not at all original with Marx.

The second supposed novelty consisted in the discovery that "in every historical epoch, the prevailing mode of economic production and exchange, and the social organization necessarily following from it, form the basis upon which is built up, and from which alone can be explained, the political and intellectual history of that epoch." The economic explanation of society and history had been expounded before Marx by Saint-Simon, Comte, Louis Blanc, Julius Froebel, Karl Wilhelm Nitsch, and Ludwig Feuerbach; it goes back to Aristotle's *Politics* (book I, chapter 8). Marx undoubtedly stressed this idea more than any of his predecessors, but at the same time he failed to prove it, especially in the dogmatic version according to which the mode of production and exchange *alone* can explain political and intellectual history. That economic factors—of which the mode of production and exchange is only one—exert their influence on all other elements of social life and, in turn, are influenced by those elements, has become a truism of modern science. Marx was guilty of making a sweeping and untenable generalization. But we must give him credit for having emphasized the importance of economic factors at a time when the social sciences generally were ignoring their crucial impact.

Redemption of the Living Mortals

Marx's third original idea, according to Engels, was that under modern conditions the oppressed class, the proletariat, "cannot attain its emancipation from the sway of the exploiting and ruling class—the bourgeoisie —without, at the same time, and once and for all, emancipating society at large from all exploitation, oppression, class-distinctions and class struggles." The revolutionary potential of impoverished laborers had been stressed before Marx (if we restrict ourselves to the second third of the 19th century), by Georg Buechner and Wilhelm Weitling. The historical role of the proletariat (a term invented by Mallet du Pan, a French royalist, in 1792 and later employed by Saint-Simon) had been analyzed for the first time in 1842 by Lorenz von Stein, in a work with which Marx was familiar.

The thesis, however, that the proletarian emancipation *by necessity* must bring about the perpetual "emancipation" of society as a whole is undoubtedly Marx's intellectual property. It is the revolutionary myth at its purest and strongest, logically in a class with the Pan-Slavic claim that the Slavs are destined to accomplish a universal mission, and with Bismarck's assertion that German *Wesen* would save the world. Not the slightest particle of proof is offered by Marx for this promise of secular redemption. Nor does he bother to indicate what organizational measures this abstraction, the proletariat, is to take in order to do away with exploitation and oppression. Marx is really saying that once the proletariat has accomplished a successful revolution, human history with all its conflicts will come to an end and the millennium will be realized on earth. It is a modern radical's re-write of St. Augustine's *inquietum est cor nostrum, donec requiescat in te;* and a revolutionary and activist interpretation of Hegel's "periods of harmony, periods when the antithesis is in abeyance." Evidently, such *secularized Messianism* has no proper place in a doctrine which calls itself "scientific."

THE MANIFESTO'S AUTHORSHIP: MARX OR MARX-AND-ENGELS?

The effectiveness of the *Manifesto* undoubtedly is due, in large part, to the vigor and brilliance with which Marx expounded ideas for which his audience had been preconditioned emotionally. Perhaps it is unfair to judge the accomplishment of Marx on the basis of the originality of the individual component ideas. His assignment was to produce a synthesis, and it can be argued that it is the originality of his synthesis which ought to be evaluated. Very well. But first, was it Marx's own synthesis? While Marx was using Engels' *Foundations* as a first draft, and probably also consulted Hess' contribution, the differences between the *Manifesto* and those other works are so great that Marx must be considered as *the* author of the *Communist Manifesto*. One suspects, indeed, that the socialist and communist parties have tried to suppress Engels' *Foundations*, since otherwise they would have taken the course of publishing them together, accrediting each to its proper author.

MARX VERSUS ENGELS

Though only a hastily drawn-up manuscript, the *Foundations* may serve as a yardstick with which to appraise the cogency of the *Manifesto's* synthesis. The *Manifesto* is a far more hate-filled and aggressive document, and as such it is a better ideological *weapon* than the *Foundations*. Yet it skips many points which Engels developed and which should have been considered in a revolutionary catechism. For example, Engels presented a far more accurate and meaningful diagnosis of the social conditions of the proletariat. He enlarged on the really crucial question of how socialist society ought to be organized. Engels here followed the path of Saint-Simon and Considérant, but at least he discussed the key problem which—rather dishonestly—Marx almost entirely ignored. Engels identified many social reforms and, throughout the entire document, displayed awareness of the need for gradual change.

The two documents set forth roughly the same concrete program, except that Engels spoke of *limiting* private property, the *gradual* expropriation of land property, the paying of indemnities for expropriated property, the competition of state-owned and privately owned enterprises, the need for labor to organize, and the need to provide decent housing for the poor. He acknowledged that peaceful change would be desirable, though he did not deny that violent change may be inevitable. All these are significant differences between the *Foundations* and the *Manifesto*.

THE "PROGRAM"

A few further observations must be made about the specific "program" of the *Communist Manifesto*. To begin with, many of these "revolutionary" measures are, and always have been, standard items in the reform schedules of all modern nations. All civilized countries now offer free education. It is the countries with the most developed free enterprise system and with the most pronounced democratic form of government that offer the best and cheapest education to the largest number of people. Civilized nations also forbid child labor, and by now they have done away with it almost entirely. (Such labor is being eliminated rapidly even in backward colonial areas, where, however, children do not work in factories.) Most civilized nations have progressive taxes, and it is noteworthy that Soviet Russia has a far less gradated income tax than the United States. Soil improvement and conservation have become routine jobs of modern governments. Most European nations have centralized the means of communication and transport in the hands of the state—but American private communication and transport industries have been able to offer better and cheaper services. While communists and socialists have always held that the state will, as a matter of course, do a good job as economic organizer, they have held this in the teeth of the evidence. They have, moreover, contented themselves with the *magic* quality of the idea and never have really tried to explain *how* a state ought to be organized to do a reliably good job of economic management. Nor have they bothered their heads about the limits beyond which a state cannot act effectively as an economic decision-maker. Would it not make better sense, before proposing revolution and bloodshed, to *prove* the contention that only the state is capable of organizing society effectively and that an economy run by the state is the most productive and the most equitable? Is it not strange that the defenders of feudalism also believed in the insuperable wisdom of the state?

The communists have *never yet* presented useful and original reform ideas. They have simply pilfered—and distorted—the liberal and conservative-liberal reform programs; or emulated out-of-date and discredited feudalistic concepts. In advocating the abolition of private property, however, the *Communist Manifesto* departed from liberal and conservative reform schemes. Yet Marx did not stop to examine the usefulness of the proposed measure. He did not even array the anti-property arguments of earlier socialists but, strangely enough, pussyfooted: merely the abolition of property in *land* was recommended. By implication, all other types of private property were to remain intact, to the extent that they could survive progressive taxation and the abolition of inheritance rights.

Only in the very end are all "instruments of production" to be concentrated "in the hands of the state, i.e. of the proletariat organized as the ruling class." The term "instruments of production" is not defined, but the admission that there will be, after all, a "ruling class," is most interesting. How the state with the proletariat as its ruling class will transform itself into a "vast association of the whole nation" (an idea borrowed from Fourier), and how then "public power will lose its political character" (shades of Proudhon!) is left to the imagination of the true believer. The state as organizer of production (a concept from Saint-Simon), hardly can be anything but a public and political institution —or is industry going to be returned to *private* management once the present property-holders have been liquidated? Marx was noncommittal about the future, not because, as he pretended, it is unscientific to make predictions—he made many predictions—but because he did not know how to organize a workable and truly emancipatory socialist society. After more than one hundred years, his disciples still are in the same fix.

SOCIALISM AND SLAVE LABOR

The greatest mystery of why so-called "progressives" embrace Marxian communism is provided by the *Manifesto's* proposal regarding "equal liability of all to labor" and the "establishment of industrial armies especially for agriculture." This phrasing is an identical re-write of Engels' formula in the *Foundations,* except that after the word "labor" Engels had added the following: "until the total suppression of private property." Thus, Engels proposed slave labor as a transitory measure, presumably as a method of forcing the idle, the rich and the non-proletarians to do manual labor. By contrast, the *Manifesto* advocated compulsory labor service on a *permanent* basis. Let it be clearly understood, then, that communism, on the strength of its own demands, must be built upon slave labor. This was pointed out as early as 1848 by de Tocqueville, who said that the socialist state inevitably must become the master of each man. Socialism "is the confiscation . . . of human liberty. . . . It is serfdom under a new formula." How, we may ask, did such a system ever come to be regarded as "progressive"?

The communists who still uphold the *Manifesto* as their gospel cannot be accused of inconsistency: they do operate slave labor camps. The social democrats and socialists oppose the communists on this point very strongly. But they have never clearly repudiated the Marxian program. It is true that they adhere to Marx only in a dilatory fashion. But as late as 1948 even the British Labor Party published a centennial edition of the *Manifesto,* in which Harold Laski failed to take issue with the proposed introduction of slave labor.

Karl Kautsky, to this day the leading theoretician of socialism, wrote in his *Grundsaetze und Forderungen der Sozialdemokratie* (1892) as follows:

> Socialist production is not compatible with liberty of work; that is to say, with the worker's freedom to work when or how he likes.
> . . . It is true that under the rule of capitalism, a worker still enjoys liberty up to a certain degree. If he does not quite like a factory, he can find work elsewhere. In a socialist society, all the means of production will be concentrated in the hands of the state, and the latter

will be the only employer; there will be no choice. The workman today enjoys more liberty than he will possess in a socialist society.

To "repudiate" Engels, Marx and Kautsky on this central point is not good enough. For once, these men were right: socialism without compulsory labor is as impossible as wooden iron or dry water. Is it not time for the labor movement to acknowledge that socialism is a false solution to the problems of misery and oppression? Is it not obvious that freedom and well-being cannot be accomplished by the abolition of property, but only by maintaining or creating conditions in which the largest number of citizens are able to acquire property and, through it, economic security? What must be repudiated is not just slave labor, but socialism itself.

THE COMMUNITY OF WOMEN IN TWO VERSIONS

To return to our comparison of Marx and Engels. Let us consider a concrete example. Engels took up the accusation that the communists were proposing to introduce the community of women. He reasoned that once private property were abolished, the dependence of women upon men would cease. He asserted that the community of women is typical of existing society where it is represented by prostitution. But the disappearance of private property would spell the end of prostitution also.

What did Marx make of this rather sober statement? He explained that the bourgeois sees "in his wife a mere instrument of production," and consequently exploits her like any other instrument of production. According to Marx, the community of women exists because in addition to having access to prostitutes, the bourgeois abuse the wives and daughters of the proletarians, and moreover seduce each others' wives. Thus, "bourgeois marriage is in reality a system of wives in common." * Accordingly, the communists could be reproached only for intending to introduce "in substitution for a hypocritically

* That the 19th century was the first period of human history when to an ever increasing extent marriage became linked to romantic love, and when economic and status considerations ceded all along the line to mutual compatibility, apparently escaped the attention of our keen social critic.

concealed, an openly legalized community of women."

What Marx did to Engels' statement thus becomes clear: he transformed a point of social criticism into revolutionary ammunition. In doing so, he exaggerated the original argument and distorted the basic facts beyond recognition. At the same time, he was studiously noncommittal about his true objective. In the end, we do not know whether he was for or against the community of women in a communist society. And it is unlikely that Marx's vagueness was unintentional.

Engels' *Foundations* is free of the numerous violations of logic with which Marx weighted down the *Manifesto*. Marx informs us, for example, that since the price of labor is equal to its cost of production, "in proportion therefore, as the repulsiveness of the work increases, the wage decreases," which is obviously nonsense.

The *Foundations* is also relatively free of misstatements of fact, such as that an economic crisis leads to the "enforced destruction of a mass of productive forces," that laborers "live only so long as they find work," that "the more modern industry becomes developed, the more is the labor of men superseded by that of women," and that "in proportion as the use of machinery and division of labor increases, in the same proportion the burden of toil also increases." And Engels steered clear of pearls of balderdash like this one: "In bourgeois society . . . the past dominates the present; in communist society, the present dominates the past." All in all, it is highly doubtful whether the synthesis of the *Manifesto* really can bear comparison with the synthesis of the *Foundations*.

MARX AND CONSIDÉRANT

It is useful to compare the *Manifesto* with another contemporary synthesis, Victor Considérants *Principes du Socialisme,* first published in 1843 and re-issued in 1847. The structure of the *Manifesto* resembles that of the *Principes* to such a point that Marx has been accused of plagiarizing Considérant. This is unjust—if only Marx had borrowed from Considérant!

Considérant did not content himself with making a diagnosis of social ills. He was interested in solutions, not for revolution's sake, but in order to improve society. He left no doubt that a situation in which poverty was spreading rapidly could not last. If existing society was doomed, it would have to be replaced either by communism or by cooperation. He rejected the revolutionary solution because it must be violent and forever illusionary; and because stability, the conservation of order, and respect for historical tradition, have the *primary and basic* conditions of healthy social life. Not that he disputed the merits of progress; but progress can be achieved only within the going concern of a stable and basically satisfactory social order.

Considérant attacked Rousseau's proposal that private property be abolished. Instead he proposed a program of social progress without revolution, wide distribution of wealth, and the realization of order, justice and freedom, all of this to be achieved through the organization of industry and the voluntary association of capital, labor and talent.

Admittedly, Considérant's solutions were vague in many respects. Yet by contrast to

Marx, he was on the right track. He tackled the problem from a greater number of important angles than Marx ever perceived. Under different names and slogans, and in varying degrees, Western societies *have* brought together labor, capital and talent. They *have* succeeded in making the poor, not rich, but richer. History has approved of Considérant's concepts.

It has been said often that Marx must have been right because his predictions were accurate. Nothing could be more untrue, as witness this extraordinary morsel:

> The modern laborer . . . instead of rising with the progress of industry sinks deeper and deeper below the conditions of existence of his own class. . . . The bourgeoisie is unfit any longer to be the ruling class in society . . . because it is incompetent to assure an existence to its slave within his slavery, because it cannot help letting him sink into such a state that it has to feed him, instead of being fed by him.

Marx and Religion

A last point of comparison. Marx affirmed that the charges against communism made from a religious standpoint "are not deserving of serious examination." Since man's consciousness allegedly changes with the conditions of his material existence, religious ideas must change with the coming of the communist revolution, which will involve "the most radical rupture with traditional ideas." Christian ideals, he insisted, "succumbed in the 18th century to rationalist ideas"—another choice sample of historical diagnosis. And, as is well known, Marx believed in general that religious doctrines are fabrications the function of which is to veil economic exploitation. All of which is double-talk, behind which is concealed the intent of doing away with Christianity.

Considérant, by contrast, pointed out that it is an illusion to think that Christianity can be replaced by a *better* religion. "The individual and collective union of men with one another and their individual and collective union with God: there never will be a higher religious principle. This principle is that of Christianity." Considérant emphasized that the most lofty ideals of political and social reform are nothing but manifestations of the spirit of Christ. "Christianity which broke the chains of slaves . . . has only begun to accomplish its mission." It is this central connection between religion, reform, and political organization which Marx failed so utterly to understand: that social structures will conform to the ideas of mankind only if their members, and especially their rulers, are imbued with Christian (or at least with advanced religious) concepts. Millions of freeborn Russians wasting away in communist labor camps and numerous American prisoners of war who have suffered the ordeal of brain-washing testify to the inhuman hopelessness of a state in which this spirit is lacking. From theocide through liberticide to genocide—this is a historical "law" which Marx omitted from his considerations.

The synthesis of the *Communist Manifesto* was a long step backward on the road of human progress. The world should rue the day when, through a series of historical accidents, labor movements and "progressive" intellectuals adopted Marxist communism as their program and intellectual tool, and with it its Marxian trickery, dishonesty, blindness, and lack of objectivity, even while they were discarding more mature systems of social reform. The undisputed literary success of the *Communist Manifesto* is not due to its merits of thought. Its popularity does not spring from a free intellectual competition between reform concepts. It is the result of an artificially created monopoly in a particular field of thought. It is due to the fact that the pamphlet has been disseminated as an *organizational* document. And the tragedy is that there still are organizations committed to its worship. Truly, many among us have nothing to lose but their intellectual chains. They have a world to win—where reason can be applied to advance the cause of human progress and freedom; and where the imperishable ideals of the True, the Good and the Beautiful again can be professed freely without hindrance from a false, intolerant and witless creed which its originator, deep in his own conscience, himself probably did not take seriously.

STEFAN T. POSSONY
Georgetown University

Feb. 27, 1954

Communist

Manifesto

PREFACE

THE "MANIFESTO" was published as the platform of the "Communist League," a working-
men's association, first exclusively German,
later on international, and under the political
conditions of the Continent before 1848, un-
avoidably a secret society. At a Congress of
the League, held in London in November,
1847, Marx and Engels were commissioned
to prepare for publication a complete theoretical and practical party-program. Drawn
up in German, in January, 1848, the manuscript was sent to the printer in London a
few weeks before the French revolution of
February 24th. A French translation was
brought out in Paris, shortly before the insurrection of June, 1848. The first English
translation, by Miss Helen Macfarlane, appeared in George Julian Harney's "Red Republican," London, 1850. A Danish and a
Polish edition had also been published.

The defeat of the Parisian insurrection of
June, 1848—the first great battle between
Proletariat and Bourgeoisie—drove again

1

into the background, for a time, the social and political aspirations of the European working class. Thenceforth, the struggle for supremacy was again, as it had been before the revolution of February, solely between different sections of the propertied class; the working class was reduced to a fight for political elbow-room, and to the position of extreme wing of the Middle-Class Radicals. Wherever independent proletarian movements continued to show signs of life, they were ruthlessly hunted down. Thus the Prussian police hunted out the Central Board of the Communist League, then located in Cologne. The members were arrested, and, after eighteen months' imprisonment, they were tried in October, 1852. This celebrated "Cologne Communist trial" lasted from October 4th till November 12th; seven of the prisoners were sentenced to terms of imprisonment in a fortress, varying from three to six years. Immediately after the sentence the League was formally dissolved by the remaining members. As to the "Manifesto," it seemed thenceforth to be doomed to oblivion.

When the European working class had recovered sufficient strength for another attack

2

on the ruling classes, the International Working Men's Association sprang up. But this association, formed with the express aim of welding into one body the whole militant proletariat of Europe and America, could not at once proclaim the principles laid down in the "Manifesto." The International was bound to have a program broad enough to be acceptable to the English Trades' Union, to the followers of Proudhon in France, Belgium, Italy and Spain, and to the Lassalleans[1] in Germany. Marx, who drew up this program to the satisfaction of all parties, entirely trusted to the intellectual development of the working-class, which was sure to result from combined action and mutual discussion. The very events and vicissitudes of the struggle against Capital, the defeats even more than the victories, could not help bringing home to men's minds the insufficiency of their various favorite nostrums, and preparing the

1. Lassalle personally, to us, always acknowledged himself to be a disciple of Marx, and, as such, stood on the ground of the "Manifesto." But in his public agitation, 1860-64, he did not go beyond demanding co-operative workshops supported by State credit.

3

way for a more complete insight into the true conditions of working-class emancipation. And Marx was right. The International, on its breaking up in 1874, left the workers quite different men from what it had found them in 1864. Proudhonism in France, Lassalleanism in Germany were dying out, and even the Conservative English Trades' Unions, though most of them had long since severed their connection with the International were gradually advancing towards that point at which, last year at Swansea, their president could say in their name, "Continental Socialism has lost its terrors for us." In fact, the principles of the "Manifesto" had made considerable headway among the working men of all countries.

The "Manifesto" itself thus came to the front again. The German text had been, since 1850, reprinted several times in Switzerland, England and America. In 1872, it was translated into English in New York, where the translation was published in "Woodhull and Claflin's Weekly." From this English version, a French one was made in "Le Socialiste" of New York. Since then at least two more English translations, more or less mutilated, have

4

been brought out in America, and one of
them has been reprinted in England. The
first Russian translation made by Bakounin,
was published at Herzen's "Kolokol" office in
Geneva, about 1863; a second one, by the
heroic Vera Zasulitch, also in Geneva, 1882.
A new Danish edition is to be found in "So-
cialdemokratisk Bibliothek," Copenhagen,
1885; a fresh French translation in "Le Socialiste," Paris, 1886. From this latter a Span-
ish version was prepared and published in
Madrid, 1886. The German reprints are not
to be counted, there have been twelve altogether at the least. An Armenian translation,
which was to be published in Constantinople
some months ago, did not see the light, I am
told, because the publisher was afraid of
bringing out a book with the name of Marx
on it, while the translator declined to call it
his own production. Of further translations
into other languages I have heard, but have
not seen them. Thus the history of the Manifesto reflects, to a great extent, the history of
the modern working-class movement; at present it is undoubtedly the most widespread,
the most international production of all Socialist literature, the common platform ac-

knowledged by millions of working men from Siberia to California.

Yet, when it was written, we could not have called it a Socialist Manifesto. By Socialists, in 1847, were understood, on the one hand, the adherents of the various Utopian systems: Owenites in England, Fourierists in France, both of them already reduced to the position of mere sects, and gradually dying out; on the other hand, the most multifarious social quacks, who, by all manners of tinkering, professed to redress, without any danger to capital and profit, all sorts of social grievances, in both cases men outside the working-class movement, and looking rather to the "educated" classes for support. Whatever portion of the working class had become convinced of the insufficiency of mere political revolutions, and had proclaimed the necessity of a total social change, that portion, then, called itself Communist. It was a crude, rough-hewn, purely instinctive sort of Communism; still, it touched the cardinal point and was powerful enough amongst the working class to produce the Utopian Communism, in France, of Cabet, and in Germany, of Weitling. Thus, Socialism was in 1847, a middle-class movement, Communism a working-class movement. Socialism was, on the Continent at least, "respectable"; Communism was the very opposite. And as our notion, from the very beginning, was that "the emancipation of the working class must be the act of the working class itself," there could be no doubt as to which of the two names we must take. Moreover, we have, ever since, been far from repudiating it.

The "Manifesto" being our joint production, I consider myself bound to state that the fundamental proposition which forms its nucleus, belongs to Marx. That proposition is: that in every historical epoch, the prevailing mode of economic production and exchange, and the social organization necessarily following from it, form the basis upon which is built up, and from which alone can be explained, the political and intellectual history of that epoch; that consequently the whole history of mankind (since the dissolution of primitive tribal society, holding land in common ownership) has been a history of class struggles, contests between exploiting and exploited, ruling and oppressed classes; that the history of these class struggles forms a

7

series of evolution in which, now-a-days, a stage has been reached where the exploited and oppressed class—the proletariat—cannot attain its emancipation from the sway of the exploiting and ruling class—the bourgeoisie —without, at the same time, and once and for all, emancipating society at large from all exploitation, oppression, class-distinctions and class struggles.

This proposition which, in my opinion, is destined to do for history what Darwin's theory has done for biology, we, both of us, had been gradually approaching for some years before 1845. How far I had independently progressed towards it, is best shown by my "Conditions of the Working Class in England." [2] But when I again met Marx at Brussels in spring, 1845, he had it already worked out, and put it before me, in terms almost as clear as those in which I have stated it here.

From our joint preface to the German edition of 1872, I quote the following:

"However much the state of things may

2. The Condition of the Working Class in England in 1844, by Frederick Engels. Translated by Florence K. Wischnewetzky—London, Swan, Sonnenschein & Co.

have altered during the last 25 years, the general principles laid down in this Manifesto, are, on the whole, as correct today as ever. Here and there some detail might be improved. The practical application of the principles will depend as the Manifesto itself states, everywhere and at all times, on the historical conditions for the time being existing, and, for that reason, no special stress is laid on the revolutionary measures proposed at the end of Section II. That passage would, in many respects, be very differently worded today. In view of the gigantic strides of Modern Industry since 1848, and of the accompanying improved and extended organization of the working-class, in view of the practical experience gained, first in the February revolution, and then, still more, in the Paris Commune, where the proletariat for the first time held political power for two whole months, this program has in some details become antiquated. One thing especially was proven by the Commune, viz., that "the working-class cannot simply lay hold of the ready-made state machinery, and wield it for its own purposes." (See "The Civil War in France; Address of the General Council of the International Working Men's Association," Chicago, Charles H. Kerr & Co., where this point is further developed.) Further, it is self-evident, that the criticism of socialist literature is deficient in relation to the present time, because it comes down only to 1847; also, that the remarks on the relation of the Communists to the various opposition-parties (Section IV), although in principle still correct, yet in practice are antiquated, because the political situation has been entirely changed, and the progress of history has swept off the earth the greater portion of the political parties there enumerated.

"But then, the Manifesto has become a historical document which we have no longer any right to alter."

The present translation is by Mr. Samuel Moore, the translator of the greater portion of Marx's "Capital." We have revised it in common, and I have added a few notes explanatory of historical allusions.

FREDERICK ENGELS
London, 30th January, 1888

Manifesto
of the
Communist Party

A SPECTRE is haunting Europe—the spectre of Communism. All the powers of old Europe have entered into a holy alliance to exorcise this spectre; Pope and Czar, Metternich and Guizot, French Radicals and German police-spies.

Where is the party in opposition that has not been decried as communistic by its opponents in power? Where the opposition that has not hurled back the branding reproach of Communism, against the more advanced opposition parties, as well as against its reactionary adversaries?

Two things result from this fact.

I. Communism is already acknowledged by all European Powers to be itself a Power.

II. It is high time that Communists should openly, in the face of the whole world, publish their views, their aims, their tendencies, and meet this nursery tale of the Spectre of Communism with a Manifesto of the party itself.

To this end, Communists of various nationalities have assembled in London, and sketched the following manifesto, to be published in the English, French, German, Italian, Flemish and Danish languages.

I

Bourgeois and Proletarians[1]

The history of all hitherto existing society[2] is the history of class struggles.

1. By bourgeoisie is meant the class of modern Capitalists, owners of the means of social production and employers of wage-labor. By proletariat, the class of modern wage-laborers who, having no means of production of their own, are reduced to selling their labor-power in order to live.

2. That is, all written history. In 1847, the pre-history of society, the social organization existing previous to recorded history, was all but unknown. Since then, Haxthausen discovered common ownership of land in Russia, Maurer proved it to be the social foundation from which all Teutonic races started in history, and by and by village communities were found to be, or to have been, the primitive form of society everywhere from India to Ireland. The inner organiza-

Freeman and slave, patrician and plebeian, lord and serf, guild-master[3] and journeyman, in a word; oppressor and oppressed, stood in constant opposition to one another, carried on an uninterrupted, now hidden, now open fight, a fight that each time ended, either in a revolutionary re-constitution of society at large, or in the common ruin of the contending classes.

In the early epochs of history, we find almost everywhere a complicated arrangement of society into various orders, a manifold graduation of social rank. In ancient Rome we have patricians, knights, plebeians, slaves; in the Middle Ages, feudal lords, vassals, guild-masters, journeymen, apprentices, serfs;

tion of this primitive Communistic society was laid bare, in its typical form, by Morgan's crowning discovery of the true nature of the gens and its relation to the tribe. With the dissolution of these primeval communities society begins to be differentiated into separate and finally antagonistic classes. I have attempted to retrace this process of dissolution in "The Origin of the Family, Private Property and the State." (Chicago, Charles H. Kerr & Co.)

3. Guild-master, that is a full member of a guild, a master within, not a head of, a guild.

14

in almost all of these classes, again, subordinate gradations.

The modern bourgeois society that has sprouted from the ruins of feudal society, has not done away with class antagonisms. It has but established new classes, new conditions of oppression, new forms of struggle in place of the old ones.

Our epoch, the epoch of the bourgeoisie, possesses, however, this distinctive feature; it has simplified the class antagonisms. Society as a whole is more and more splitting up into two great hostile camps, into two great classes directly facing each other: Bourgeoisie and Proletariat.

From the serfs of the Middle Ages sprang the chartered burghers of the earliest towns. From these burgesses the first elements of the bourgeoisie were developed.

The discovery of America, the rounding of the Cape, opened up fresh ground for the rising bourgeoisie. The East-Indian and Chinese markets, the colonization of America, trade with the colonies, the increase in the means of exchange and in commodities, generally, gave to commerce, to navigation, to industry, an impulse never before known, and thereby, to the revolutionary element in the tottering feudal society, a rapid development.

The feudal system of industry, under which industrial production was monopolized by closed guilds, now no longer sufficed for the growing wants of the markets. The manufacturing system took its place. The guild-masters were pushed on one side by the manufacturing middle-class; division of labor between the different corporate guilds vanished in the face of division of labor in each single workshop.

Meantime the markets kept ever growing, the demand, ever rising. Even manufacturing no longer sufficed. Thereupon, steam and machinery revolutionized industrial production. The place of manufacture was taken by the giant, Modern Industry, the place of the industrial middle-class, by industrial millionaires, the leaders of whole industrial armies, the modern bourgeoisie.

Modern Industry has established the world-market, for which the discovery of America paved the way. This market has given an immense development to commerce, to navigation, to communication by land.

This development has, in its turn, reacted on the extension of industry; and in proportion as industry, commerce, navigation, railways extended in the same proportion the bourgeoisie developed, increased its capital, and pushed into the background every class handed down from the Middle Ages.

We see, therefore, how the modern bourgeoisie is itself the product of a long course of development, of a series of revolutions in the modes of production and of exchange.

Each step in the development of the bourgeoisie was accompained by a corresponding political advance of that class. An oppressed class under the sway of the feudal nobility, an armed and self-governing association in the medieval commune,[4] here independent urban republic (as in Italy and Germany), there taxable "third estate" of the monarchy (as in France), afterwards, in the period of

4. "Commune" was the name taken, in France, by the nascent towns even before they had conquered from their feudal lords and masters, local self-government and political rights as "the Third Estate." Generally speaking, for the economical development of the bourgeoisie, England is here taken as the typical country; for its political development, France.

manufacturing proper, serving either the semi-feudal or the absolute monarchy as a counterpoise against the nobility, and in fact, cornerstone of the great monarchies in general, the bourgeoisie has at last, since the establishment of Modern Industry and of the world-market, conquered for itself, in the modern representative State, exclusive political sway. The executive of the modern State is but a committee for managing the common affairs of the whole bourgeoisie.

The bourgeoisie, historically, has played a most revolutionary part.

The bourgeoisie, wherever it has got the upper hand, has put an end to all feudal, patriarchal, idyllic relations. It has pitilessly torn asunder the motley feudal ties that bound man to his "natural superiors," and has left remaining no other nexus between man and man than naked self-interest, than callous "cash payment." It has drowned the most heavenly ecstasies of religious fervor, of chivalrous enthusiasm, of philistine sentimentalism, in the icy water of egotistical calculation. It has resolved personal worth into exchange value, and in place of the numberless indefeasible chartered freedoms, has set up that single, unconscionable freedom—Free Trade. In one word, for exploitation, veiled by religious and political illusions, it has substituted naked, shameless, direct, brutal exploitation.

The bourgeoisie has stripped of its halo every occupation hitherto honored and looked up to with reverent awe. It has converted the physician, the lawyer, the priest, the poet, the man of science, into its paid wage-laborers.

The bourgeoisie has torn away from the family its sentimental veil, and has reduced the family relation to a mere money relation.

The bourgeoisie has disclosed how it came to pass that the brutal display of vigor in the Middle Ages, which Reactionists so much admire, found its fitting complement in the most slothful indolence. It has been the first to show what man's activity can bring about. It has accomplished wonders far surpassing Egyptian pyramids, Roman aqueducts, and Gothic cathedrals; it has conducted expeditions that put in the shade all former Exoduses of nations and crusades.

The bourgeoisie cannot exist without constantly revolutionizing the instruments of production, and thereby the relations of production, and with them the whole relations of society. Conservation of the old modes of production in unaltered form, was, on the contrary, the first condition of existence for all earlier industrial classes. Constant revolutionizing of production, uninterrupted disturbance of all social conditions, everlasting uncertainty and agitation distinguish the bourgeois epoch from all earlier ones. All fixed, fast-frozen relations, with their train of ancient and venerable prejudices and opinions, are swept away, all newly-formed ones become antiquated before they can ossify. All that is solid melts into air, all that is holy is profaned, and man is at last compelled to face with sober senses, his real conditions of life, and his relations with his kind.

The need of a constantly expanding market for its products chases the bourgeoisie over the whole surface of the globe. It must nestle everywhere, settle everywhere, establish connections everywhere.

The bourgeoisie has through its exploitation of the world-market given a cosmopolitan character to production and consumption in every country. To the great chagrin of Reactionists, it has drawn from under the feet of industry the national ground on which it stood. All old-established national industries have been destroyed or are daily being destroyed. They are dislodged by new industries, whose introduction becomes a life and death question for all civilized nations, by industries that no longer work up indigenous raw material, but raw material drawn from the remotest zones; industries whose products are consumed, not only at home, but in every quarter of the globe. In place of the old wants, satisfied by the productions of the country, we find new wants, requiring for their satisfaction the products of distant lands and climes. In place of the old local and national seclusion and self-sufficiency, we have intercourse in every direction, universal interdependence of nations. And as in material, so also in intellectual production. The intellectual creations of individual nations become common property. National one-sidedness and narrow-mindedness become more and more impossible, and from the numerous national and local literatures there arises a world-literature.

The bourgeoisie, by the rapid improvement

of all instruments of production, by the immensely facilitated means of communication, draws all, even the most barbarian, nations into civilization. The cheap prices of its commodities are the heavy artillery with which it batters down all Chinese walls, with which it forces the barbarians' intensely obstinate hatred of foreigners to capitulate. It compels all nations, on pain of extinction, to adopt the bourgeois mode of production; it compels them to introduce what it calls civilization into their midst, i.e., to become bourgeois themselves. In a word, it creates a world after its own image.

The bourgeoisie has subjected the country to the rule of the towns. It has created enormous cities, has greatly increased the urban population as compared with the rural, and has thus rescued a considerable part of the population from the idiocy of rural life. Just as it has made the country dependent on the towns, so it has made barbarian and semibarbarian countries dependent on the civilized ones, nations of peasants on nations of bourgeois, the East on the West.

The bourgeoisie keeps more and more doing away with the scattered state of the population, of the means of production, and of property. It has agglomerated population, centralized means of production, and has concentrated property in a few hands. The necessary consequence of this was political centralization. Independent, or but loosely connected provinces, with separate interests, laws, governments and systems of taxation, became lumped together in one nation, with one government, one code of laws, one national class-interest, one frontier and one customs-tariff.

The bourgeoisie, during its rule of scarce one hundred years, has created more massive and more colossal productive forces than have all preceding generations together. Subjection of Nature's forces to man, machinery, application of chemistry to industry and agriculture, steam-navigation, railways, electric telegraphs, clearing of whole continents for cultivation, canalization of rivers, whole populations conjured out of the ground—what earlier century had even a presentiment that such productive forces slumbered in the lap of social labor?

We see then: the means of production and of exchange on whose foundations the bourgeoisie built itself up, were generated in feudal society. At a certain stage in the development of these means of production and of exchange, the conditions under which feudal society produced and exchanged, the feudal organization of agriculture and manufacturing industry, in one word, the feudal relations of property became no longer compatible with the already developed productive forces; they became so many fetters. They had to be burst asunder; they were burst asunder.

Into their places stepped free competition, accompanied by a social and political constitution adapted to it, and by the economical and political sway of the bourgeois class.

A similar movement is going on before our own eyes. Modern bourgeois society with its relations of production, of exchange and of property, a society that has conjured up such gigantic means of production and of exchange, is like the sorcerer, who is no longer able to control the power of the nether world whom he has called up by his spells. For many a decade past the history of industry and commerce is but the history of the revolt of modern productive forces against modern conditions of production, against the property relations that are the condition for the existence of the bourgeoisie and of its rule. It is enough to mention the commercial crises that by their periodical return put on trial, each time more threateningly, the existence of the entire bourgeois society. In these crises a great part not only of the existing products, but also of the previously created productive forces, are periodically destroyed. In these crises there breaks out an epidemic that, in all earlier epochs, would have seemed an absurdity—the epidemic of over-production. Society suddenly finds itself put back into a state of momentary barbarism; it appears as if a famine, a universal war of devastation had cut off the supply of every means of subsistence; industry and commerce seem to be destroyed; and why? Because there is too much civilization, too much means of subsistence, too much industry, too much commerce. The productive forces at the disposal of society no longer tend to further the development of the conditions of bourgeois property; on the contrary, they have become too powerful for these conditions, by which they are fettered, and so soon as they overcome these fetters, they bring disorder into the whole of bourgeois society, endangering the existence of bourgeois property. The conditions of bourgeois society are too narrow to comprise the wealth created by them. And how does the bourgeoisie get over these crises? On the one hand by enforced destruction of a mass of productive forces; on the other, by the conquest of new markets, and by the more thorough exploitation of the old ones. That is to say, by paving the way for more extensive and more destructive crises, and by diminishing the means whereby crises are prevented.

The weapons with which the bourgeoisie felled feudalism to the ground are now turned against the bourgeoisie itself.

But not only has the bourgeoisie forged the weapons that bring death to itself; it has also called into existence the men who are to wield those weapons—the modern working-class—the proletarians.

In proportion as the bourgeoisie, i.e., capital, is developed, in the same proportion is the proletariat, the modern working-class, developed, a class of laborers, who live only so long as they find work, and who find work only so long as their labor increases capital.

These laborers, who must sell themselves piecemeal, are a commodity, like every other article of commerce, and are consequently exposed to all the vicissitudes of competition, to all the fluctuations of the market.

Owing to the extensive use of machinery and to division of labor, the work of the proletarians has lost all individual character, and, consequently, all charm for the workman. He becomes an appendage of the machine, and it is only the most simple, most monotonous, and most easily acquired knack that is required of him. Hence, the cost of production of a workman is restricted, almost entirely, to the means of subsistence that he requires for his maintenance, and for the propagation of his race. But the price of a commodity, and also of labor, is equal to its cost of production. In proportion, therefore, as the repulsiveness of the work increases, the wage decreases. Nay more, in proportion as the use of machinery and division of labor increases, in the same proportion the burden of toil also increases, whether by prolongation of the working hours, by increase of the work enacted in a given time, or by increased speed of the machinery, etc.

Modern Industry has converted the little workshop of the patriarchal master into the great factory of the industrial capitalist. Masses of laborers, crowded into the factory, are organized like soldiers. As privates of the industrial army they are placed under the command of a perfect hierarchy of officers and sergeants. Not only are they the slaves of the bourgeois class, and of the bourgeois State, they are daily and hourly enslaved by the machine, by the over-looker, and, above all, by the individual bourgeois manufacturer himself. The more openly this despotism proclaims gain to be its end and aim, the more petty, the more hateful and the more embittering it is.

The less the skill and exertion or strength implied in manual labor, in other words, the more modern industry becomes developed, the more is the labor of men superseded by that of women. Differences of age and sex have no longer any distinctive social validity for the working class. All are instruments of labor, more or less expensive to use, according to their age and sex.

No sooner is the exploitation of the laborer by the manufacturer so far at an end, that he receives his wages in cash, than he is set upon by the other portions of the bourgeoisie, the landlord, the shopkeeper, the pawn-broker, etc.

The low strata of the middle class—the small tradespeople, shopkeepers, and retired tradesmen generally, the handicraftsmen and peasants—all these sink gradually into the proletariat, partly because their diminutive capital does not suffice for the scale on which Modern Industry is carried on, and is swamped in the competition with the large capitalists, partly because their specialized skill is rendered worthless by new methods of production. Thus the proletariat is re-cruited from all classes of the population.

The proletariat goes through various stages of development. With its birth begins its struggle with the bourgeoisie. At first the contest is carried on by individual laborers, then by the workpeople of a factory, then by the operatives of one trade, in one locality, against the individual bourgeois who directly exploits them. They direct their attacks not against the bourgeois conditions of produc-tion, but against the instruments of produc-tion themselves; they destroy imported wares that compete with their labor, they smash to pieces machinery, they set factories ablaze, they seek to restore by force the vanished status of the workman of the Middle Ages.

At this stage the laborers still form an incoherent mass scattered over the whole country, and broken up by their mutual competition. If anywhere they unite to form more compact bodies, this is not yet the consequence of their own active union, but of the union of bourgeoisie, which class, in order to attain its own political ends, is compelled to set the whole proletariat in motion, and is moreover yet, for a time, able to do so. At this stage, therefore, the proletarians do not fight their enemies, but the enemies of their enemies, the remnants of absolute monarchy, the landowners, the non-industrial bourgeoisie, the petty bourgeoisie. Thus the whole historical movement is concentrated in the hands of the bourgeoisie; every victory so obtained is a victory for the bourgeoisie.

But with the development of industry the proletariat not only increases in number, it becomes concentrated in great masses, its strength grows, and it feels that strength more. The various interests and conditions of life within the ranks of the proletariat are more and more equalized, in proportion as machinery obliterates all distinction of labor, and nearly everywhere reduces wages to the same low level. The growing competition among the bourgeoisie, and the resulting commercial crises, make the wages of the worker ever more fluctuating. The unceasing improvement of machinery, ever more rapidly developing, makes their livelihood more and more precarious, the collisions between individual workmen and individual bourgeois take more and more the character of collision between two classes. Thereupon the workers begin to form combinations (Trades Unions) against the bourgeoisie; they club together in order to keep up the rate of wages; they found permanent associations in order to make provision beforehand for these occasional revolts. Here and there the contest breaks out into riots.

Now and then the workers are victorious, but only for a time. The real fruits of their battles lie, not in the immediate result, but in the ever expanding union of the workers. This union is helped on by the improved means of communication that are created by modern industry, and that place the workers of different localities in contact with one another. It was just this contact that was needed to centralize the numerous local struggles, all of the same character, into one national struggle between classes. But every class struggle is a political struggle. And that union, to attain which the burghers of the Middle Ages, with their miserable highways, required centuries, the modern proletarians, thanks to railways, achieve in a few years.

This organization of the proletarians into a class, and consequently into a political party, is continually being upset again by the competition between the workers themselves. But it ever rises up again, stronger, firmer, mightier. It compels legislative recognition of particular interests of the workers, by taking advantage of the divisions among the bourgeoisie itself. Thus the ten-hour bill in England was carried.

Altogether collisions between the classes of the old society further, in many ways, the course of development of the proletariat. The bourgeoisie finds itself involved in a constant battle. At first with the aristocracy; later on, with those portions of the bourgeoisie itself, whose interests have become antagonistic to the progress of industry; at all times, with the bourgeoisie of foreign countries. In all these battles it sees itself compelled to appeal to the proletariat, to ask for its help, and thus, to drag it into the political arena. The bourgeoisie itself, therefore, supplies the proletariat with its own elements of political and general education, in other words, it furnishes the proletariat with weapons for fighting the bourgeoisie.

Further, as we have already seen, entire sections of the ruling classes are, by the advance of industry, precipitated into the proletariat, or are at least threatened in their conditions of existence. These also supply the proletariat with fresh elements of enlightenment and progress.

Finally, in times when the class-struggle nears the decisive hour, the process of dissolution going on within the ruling class, in fact, within the whole range of old society, assumes such a violent, glaring character, that a small section of the ruling class cuts itself adrift, and joins the revolutionary class, the class that holds the future in its hands. Just as, therefore, at an earlier period, a section of the nobility went over to the bourgeoisie, so now a portion of the bourgeoisie goes over to the proletariat, and in particular, a portion of the bourgeois ideologists, who have raised themselves to the level of comprehending theoretically the historical movements as a whole.

Of all the classes that stand face to face with the bourgeoisie today, the proletariat alone is a really revolutionary class. The other classes decay and finally disappear in the face of Modern Industry; the proletariat is its special and essential product.

The lower middle-class, the small manufacturer, the shopkeeper, the artisan, the peasant, all these fight against the bourgeoisie, to save from extinction their existence as fractions of the middle class. They are, therefore, not revolutionary, but conservative. Nay more, they are reactionary, for they try to roll back the wheel of history. If by chance they are revolutionary, they are so, only in view of their impending transfer into the proletariat, they thus defend not their present, but their future interests, they desert their own standpoint to place themselves at that of the proletariat.

The "dangerous class," the social scum, that passively rotting mass thrown off by the lowest layers of old society, may, here and there, be swept into the movement by a proletarian revolution; its conditions of life, however, prepare it far more for the part of a bribed tool of reactionary intrigue.

In the conditions of the proletariat, those of old society at large are already virtually swamped. The proletarian is without property; his relation to his wife and children has no longer anything in common with the bourgeois family-relations; modern industrial labor, modern subjugation to capital, the same in England as in France, in America as in Germany, has stripped him of every trace of national character. Law, morality, religion, are to him so many bourgeois prejudices, behind which lurk in ambush just as many bour·geois interests.

All the preceding classes that got the upper hand, sought to fortify their already acquired status by subjecting society at large to their conditions of appropriation. The proletarians cannot become masters of the productive forces of society, except by abolishing their own previous mode of appropriation, and thereby also every other previous mode of appropriation. They have nothing of their own to secure and to fortify; their mission is to destroy all previous securities for, and insurances of, individual property.

All previous historical movements were movements of minorities, or in the interests of minorities. The proletarian movement is the self-conscious, independent movement of the immense majority, in the interest of the immense majority. The proletariat, the lowest stratum of our present society, cannot stir, cannot raise itself up, without the whole superincumbent strata of official society being sprung into the air.

Though not in substance, yet in form, the struggle of the proletariat with the bourgeoisie is at first a national struggle. The proletariat of each country must, of course, first of all settle matters with its own bourgeoisie.

In depicting the most general phases of the development of the proletariat, we traced the more or less veiled civil war, ranging within existing society, up to the point where that war breaks out into open revolution, and where the violent overthrow of the bourgeoisie lays the foundation for the sway of the proletariat.

Hitherto, every form of society has been based, as we have already seen, on the antagonism of oppressing and oppressed classes. But in order to oppress a class, certain conditions must be assured to it under which it can, at least, continue its slavish existence. The serf, in the period of serfdom, raised himself to membership in the commune, just as the petty bourgeois, under the yoke of feudal absolutism, managed to develop into a bourgeois.

The modern laborer, on the contrary, instead of rising with the progress of industry, sinks deeper and deeper below the conditions of existence of his own class. He becomes a pauper, and pauperism develops more rapidly than population and wealth. And here it becomes evident that the bourgeoisie is unfit any longer to be the ruling class in society, and to impose its conditions of existence upon society as an over-riding law. It is unfit to rule, because it is incompetent to assure an existence to its slave within his slavery, because it cannot help letting him sink into such a state that it has to feed him, instead of being fed by him. Society can no longer live under this bourgeoisie, in other words, its existence is no longer compatible with society.

The essential condition for the existence, and for the sway of the bourgeois class, is the formation and augmentation of capital; the condition for capital is wage-labor. Wage-labor rests exclusively on competition between the laborers. The advance of industry, whose involuntary promoter is the bourgeoisie, replaces the isolation of the laborers, due to competition, by their revolutionary combination, due to association. The development of Modern Industry, therefore, cuts from under its feet the very foundation on which the bourgeoisie produces and appropriates products. What the bourgeoisie therefore produces, above all, are its own grave-diggers. Its fall and the victory of the proletariat are equally inevitable.

II

Proletarians and Communists

In what relation do the Communists stand to the proletarians as a whole?

The Communists do not form a separate party opposed to other working-class parties.

They have no interest separate and apart from those of the proletariat as a whole.

They do not set up any sectarian principles of their own, by which to shape and mould the proletarian movement.

The Communists are distinguished from the other working-class parties by this only: 1. In the national struggles of the proletarians of the different countries, they point out and bring to the front the common interests of the entire proletariat independently of all nationality. 2. In the various stages of development which the struggle of the working class against the bourgeoisie has to pass through, they always and everywhere represent the interest of the movement as a whole.

The Communists, therefore, are on the one hand, practically, the most advanced and resolute section of the working-class parties of every country, that section which pushes forward all others; on the other hand, theoretically, they have over the great mass of the proletariat the advantage of clearly understanding the line of march, the conditions, and the ultimate general results of the proletarian movement.

The immediate aim of the Communists is the same as that of all the other proletarian parties; formation of the proletariat into a class, overthrow of the bourgeois supremacy, conquest of political power by the proletariat.

The theoretical conclusions of the Communists are in no way based on ideas or principles that have been invented, or discovered, by this or that would-be universal reformer.

They merely express, in general terms, actual relations springing from an existing class struggle, from a historical movement going on under our very eyes. The abolition of existing property relations is not at all a distinctive feature of Communism.

All property relations in the past have continually been subject to historical changes consequent upon the change in historical conditions.

The French Revolution, for example, abolished feudal property in favor of bourgeois property.

The distinguishing feature of Communism is not the abolition of property generally, but the abolition of bourgeois property. But modern bourgeois private property is the final and most complete expression of the system of producing and appropriating products, that is based on class antagonism, on the exploitation of the many by the few.

In this sense, the theory of the Communists may be summed up in the single sentence: Abolition of private property.

We Communists have been reproached with the desire of abolishing the right of personally acquiring property as the fruit of a man's own labor, which property is alleged to be the groundwork of all personal freedom, activity and independence.

Hard-won, self-acquired, self-earned property! Do you mean the property of the petty artisan and of the small peasant, a form of property that preceded the bourgeois form? There is no need to abolish that; the development of industry has to a great extent already destroyed it, and is still destroying it daily.

Or do you mean modern bourgeois private property?

But does wage-labor create any property for the laborer? Not a bit. It creates capital, i.e., that kind of property which exploits wage-labor, and which cannot increase except upon condition of getting a new supply of wage-labor for fresh exploitation. Property, in its present form, is based on the antagonism of capital and wage-labor. Let us examine both sides of this antagonism.

To be a capitalist, is to have not only a purely personal, but a social status in production. Capital is a collective product, and only by the united action of many members, nay, in the last resort, only by the united action of all members of society, can it be set in motion.

Capital is therefore not a personal, it is a social power.

When, therefore, capital is converted into

common property, into the property of all members of society, personal property is not thereby transformed into social property. It is only the social character of the property that is changed. It loses its class-character.

Let us now take wage-labor.

The average price of wage-labor is the minimum wage, i.e., that quantum of the means of subsistence, which is absolutely requisite to keep the laborer in bare existence as a laborer. What, therefore, the wage-laborer appropriates by means of his labor, merely suffices to prolong and reproduce a bare existence. We by no means intend to abolish this personal appropriation of the products of labor, an appropriation that is made for the maintenance and reproduction of human life, and that leaves no surplus wherewith to command the labor of others. All that we want to do away with is the miserable character of this appropriation, under which the laborer lives merely to increase capital, and is allowed to live only in so far as the interest of the ruling class requires it.

In bourgeois society, living labor is but a means to increase accumulated labor. In Communist society, accumulated labor is but a means to widen, to enrich, to promote the existence of the laborer.

In bourgeois society, therefore, the past dominates the present; in Communist society, the present dominates the past. In bourgeois society capital is independent and has individuality, while the living person is dependent and has no individuality.

And the abolition of this state of things is called by the bourgeois, abolition of individuality and freedom! And rightly so. The abolition of bourgeois individuality, bourgeois freedom is undoubtedly aimed at.

By freedom is meant, under the present bourgeois conditions of production, free trade, free selling and buying.

But if selling and buying disappears, free selling and buying disappears also. This talk about free selling and buying, and all the other "brave words" of our bourgeoisie about freedom in general, have a meaning, if any, only in contrast with restricted selling and buying, with the fettered traders of the Middle Ages, but have no meaning when opposed to the Communistic abolition of buying and selling, of the bourgeois conditions of production, and of the bourgeoisie itself.

44

You are horrified at our intending to do away with private property. But in your existing society, private property is already done away with for nine-tenths of the population; its existence for the few is solely due to its non-existence in the hands of those nine-tenths. You reproach us, therefore, with intending to do away with a form of property, the necessary condition for whose existence is, the non-existence of any property for the immense majority of society.

In one word, you reproach us with intending to do away with your property. Precisely so; that is just what we intend.

From the moment when labor can no longer be converted into capital, money, or rent, into a social power capable of being monopolized, i.e., from the moment when individual property can no longer be transformed into bourgeois property, into capital, from that moment, you say, individuality vanishes.

You must, therefore, confess that by "individual" you mean no other person than the bourgeois, than the middle-class owner of property. This person must, indeed, be swept out of the way, and made impossible.

45

Communism deprives no man of the power to appropriate the products of society: all that it does is to deprive him of the power to subjugate the labor of others by means of such appropriation.

It has been objected, that upon the abolition of private property all work will cease, and universal laziness will overtake us.

According to this, bourgeois society ought long ago to have gone to the dogs through sheer idleness; for those of its members who work, acquire nothing, and those who acquire anything, do not work. The whole of this objection is but another expression of the tautology: that there can no longer be any wage-labor when there is no longer any capital.

All objections urged against the Communistic mode of producing and appropriating material products, have in the same way, been urged against the Communistic modes of producing and appropriating intellectual products. Just as, to the bourgeois, the disappearance of class property is the disappearance of production itself, so the disappearance of class culture is to him identical with the disappearance of all culture.

That culture, the loss of which he laments, is, for the enormous majority, a mere training to act as a machine.

But don't wrangle with us so long as you apply, to our intended abolition of bourgeois property, the standard of your bourgeois notions of freedom, culture, law, etc. Your very ideas are but the outgrowth of the conditions of your bourgeois production and bourgeois property, just as your jurisprudence is but the will of your class made into a law for all, a will, whose essential character and direction are determined by the economic conditions of existence of your class.

The selfish misconception that induces you to transform into eternal laws of nature and of reason, the social forms springing from your present mode of production and form of property—historical relations that arise and disappear in the progress of production—this misconception you share with every ruling class that has preceded you. What you see clearly in the case of ancient property, what you admit in the case of feudal property, you are of course forbidden to admit in the case of your own bourgeois form of property.

Abolition of the family! Even the most

radical flare up at this infamous proposal of the Communists.

On what foundation is the present family, the bourgeois family, based? On capital, on private gain. In its completely developed form this family exists only among the bourgeoisie. But this state of things finds its complement in the practical absence of the family among the proletarians, and in public prostitution.

The bourgeois family will vanish as a matter of course when its complement vanishes, and both will vanish with the vanishing of capital.

Do you charge us with wanting to stop the exploitation of children by their parents? To this crime we plead guilty.

But, you will say, we destroy the most hallowed of relations, when we replace home education by social.

And your education! Is not that also social, and determined by the social conditions under which you educate, by the intervention, direct or indirect, of society by means of schools, etc.? The Communists have not invented the intervention of society in education; they do but seek to alter the character

48

of that intervention, and to rescue education from the influence of the ruling class.

The bourgeois clap-trap about the family and education, about the hallowed co-relation of parent and child, becomes all the more disgusting, the more, by the action of Modern Industry, all family ties among the proletarians are torn asunder, and their children transformed into simple articles of commerce and instruments of labor.

But you Communists would introduce community of women, screams the whole bourgeoisie in chorus.

The bourgeois sees in his wife a mere instrument of production. He hears that the instruments of production are to be exploited in common, and, naturally, can come to no other conclusion, than that the lot of being common to all will likewise fall to the women.

He has not even a suspicion that the real point aimed at is to do away with the status of women as mere instruments of production.

For the rest, nothing is more ridiculous than the virtuous indignation of our bourgeois at the community of women which, they pretend, is to be openly and officially established by the Communists. The Communists have

49

no need to introduce community of women; it has existed almost from time immemorial.

Our bourgeois, not content with having the wives and daughters of their proletarians at their disposal, not to speak of common prostitutes, take the greatest pleasure in seducing each others' wives.

Bourgeois marriage is in reality a system of wives in common and thus, at the most, what the Communists might possibly be reproached with, is that they desire to introduce, in substitution for a hypocritically concealed, an openly legalized community of women. For the rest, it is self-evident, that the abolition of the present system of production must bring with it the abolition of the community of women springing from that system, i.e., of prostitution both public and private.

The Communists are further reproached with desiring to abolish countries and nationalities.

The working men have no country. We cannot take away from them what they have not got. Since the proletariat must first of all acquire political supremacy, must rise to be the leading class of the nation, must constitute itself the nation, it is, so far, itself national, though not in the bourgeois sense of the word.

National differences, and antagonisms between peoples, are daily more and more vanishing, owing to the development of the bourgeoisie, to freedom of commerce, to the world-market, to uniformity in the mode of production and in the conditions of life corresponding thereto.

The supremacy of the proletariat will cause them to vanish still faster. United action, of the leading civilized countries at least, is one of the first conditions for the emancipation of the proletariat.

In proportion as the exploitation of one individual by another is put an end to, the exploitation of one nation by another will also be put an end to. In proportion as the antagonism between classes within the nation vanishes, the hostility of one nation to another will come to an end.

The charges against Communism made from a religious, a philosophical, and, generally, from an ideological standpoint, are not deserving of serious examination.

Does it require deep intuition to comprehend that man's ideas, views, and conceptions, in one word, man's consciousness, changes with every change in the condition of his material existence, in his socal relations and in his social life?

What else does the history of ideas prove, than that intellectual production changes in character in proportion as material production is changed? The ruling ideas of each age have ever been the ideas of the ruling class.

When people speak of ideas that revolutionize society, they do but express the fact, that within the old society, the elements of a new one have been created, and that the dissolution of the old ideas keeps even pace with the dissolution of the old conditions of existence.

When the ancient world was in its last throes, the ancient religions were overcome by Christianity. When Christian ideas succumbed in the 18th century to rationalist ideas, feudal society fought its death-battle with the then revolutionary bourgeoisie. The idea of religious liberty and freedom of conscience, merely gave expression to the sway of free competition within the domain of knowledge.

"Undoubtedly," it will be said, "religious,

moral, philosophical and juridical ideas have been modified in the course of historical development. But religion, morality, philosophy, political science, and law, constantly survived this change.

"There are, besides, eternal truths, such as Freedom, Justice, etc., that are common to all states of society. But Communism abolishes eternal truths, it abolishes all religion, and all morality, instead of constituting them on a new basis; it therefore acts in contradiction to all past historical experience."

What does this accusation reduce itself to? The history of all past society has consisted in the development of class antagonisms, antagonisms that assumed different forms at different epochs.

But whatever form they may have taken, one fact is common to all past ages, viz., the exploitation of one part of society by another. No wonder, then, that the social consciousness of past ages, despite all the multiplicity and variety it displays, moves within certain common forms, or general ideas, which cannot completely vanish except with the total disappearance of class antagonisms.

The Communist revolution is the most radical rupture with traditional property-relations; no wonder that its development involves the most radical rupture with traditional ideas.

We have seen above, that the first step in the revolution by the working class, is to raise the proletariat to the position of ruling class, to win the battle of democracy.

The proletariat will use its political supremacy, to wrest, by degrees, all capital from the bourgeoisie, to centralize all instruments of production in the hands of the State, i.e., of the proletariat organized as the ruling class; and to increase the total of productive forces as rapidly as possible.

Of course, in the beginning, this cannot be effected except by means of despotic inroads on the rights of property, and on the conditions of bourgeois production, by means of measures, therefore, which appear economically insufficient and untenable, but which, in the course of the movement, outstrip themselves, necessitate further inroads upon the old social order, and are unavoidable as a means of entirely revolutionizing the mode of production.

These measures will of course be different in different countries.

Nevertheless in the most advanced countries the following will be pretty generally applicable:

1. Abolition of property in land and application of all rents of land to public purposes.

2. A heavy progressive or graduated income tax.

3. Abolition of all right of inheritance.

4. Confiscation of the property of all emigrants and rebels.

5. Centralization of credit in the hands of the State, by means of a national bank with State capital and an exclusive monopoly.

6. Centralization of the means of communication and transport in the hands of the State.

7. Extension of factories and instruments of production owned by the State, the bringing into cultivation of waste lands, and the improvement of the soil generally in accordance with a common plan.

8. Equal liability of all to labor. Establishment of industrial armies, especially for agriculture.

9. Combination of agriculture with manufacturing industries; gradual abolition of the distinction between town and country, by a more equable distribution of population over the country.

10. Free education for all children in public schools. Abolition of children's factory labor in its present form. Combination of education with industrial production, etc., etc.

When, in the course of development, class distinctions have disappeared, and all production has been concentrated in the hands of a vast association of the whole nation, the public power will lose its political character. Political power, properly so called, is merely the organized power of one class for suppressing another. If the proletariat during its contest with the bourgeoisie is compelled, by the force of circumstances, to organize itself as a class, if, by means of a revolution, it makes itself the ruling class, and, as such, sweeps away by force the old conditions of production, then it will, along with these conditions, have swept away the conditions for the existence of class antagonisms, and of classes generally, and will thereby have abolished its own supremacy as a class.

In place of the old bourgeois society, with its classes and class antagonisms, we shall have an association, in which the free development of each is the condition for the free development of all.

III

SOCIALIST AND COMMUNIST LITERATURE

1. *Reactionary Socialism*
2. *Feudal Socialism*

OWING to their historical position, it became the vocation of the aristocracies of France and England to write pamphlets against modern bourgeois society. In the French revolution of July, 1830, and in the English reform agitation, these aristocracies again succumbed to the hateful upstart. Thenceforth, a serious political contest was altogether out of the question. A literary battle alone remained possible. But even in the domain of literature the old cries of the restoration period [1] had become impossible.

In order to arouse sympathy, the aristocracy were obliged to lose sight, apparently, of their own interests, and to formulate their indictment against the bourgeoisie in the interest of the exploited working class alone. Thus the aristocracy took their revenge by singing lampoons on their new master, and whispering in his ears sinister prophecies of coming catastrophe.

In this way arose feudal socialism; half lamentation, half lampoon; half echo of the past, half menace of the future; at times, by its bitter, witty and incisive criticism, striking the bourgeoisie to the very hearts' core, but always ludicrous in its effect, through total incapacity to comprehend the march of modern history.

The aristocracy, in order to rally the people to them, waved the proletarian alms-bag in front for a banner. But the people, so often as it joined them, saw on their hindquarters the

1. Not the English Restoration 1660 to 1669, but the French Restoration 1814 to 1830.

old feudal coats of arms, and deserted with loud and irreverent laughter.

One section of the French Legitimists, and "Young England," exhibited this spectacle.

In pointing out that their mode of exploitation was different to that of the bourgeoisie, the feudalists forgot that they exploited under circumstances and conditions that were quite different, and that are now antiquated. In showing that, under their rule, the modern proletariat never existed, they forget that the modern bourgeoisie is the necessary offspring of their own form of society.

For the rest, so little do they conceal the reactionary character of their criticism, that their chief accusation against the bourgeoisie amounts to this, that under the bourgeoisie regime a class is being developed, which is destined to cut up root and branch the old order of society.

What they upbraid the bourgeoisie with is not so much that it creates a proletariat, as that it creates a revolutionary proletariat.

In political practice, therefore, they join in all coercive measures against the working-class; and in ordinary life, despite their high-falutin phrases, they stoop to pick up the golden apples dropped from the tree of industry, and to barter truth, love, and honor for traffic in wool, beet-root sugar and potato spirit.[2]

As the parson has ever gone hand in hand with the landlord, so has Clerical Socialism with Feudal Socialism.

Nothing is easier than to give Christian asceticism a Socialist tinge. Has not Christianity declaimed against private property, against marriage, against the State? Has it not preached in the place of these, charity and poverty, celibacy, and mortification of the flesh, monastic life and Mother Church? Christian Socialism is but the Holy Water with which the priest consecrates the heart-burnings of the aristocrat.

2. This applies chiefly to Germany where the landed aristocracy and squirearchy have large portions of their estates cultivated for their own account by stewards, and are, moreover, extensive beet-root-sugar manufacturers and distillers of potato spirits. The wealthier British aristocracy are, as yet, rather above that; but they, too, know how to make up for declining rents by lending their names to floaters of more or less shady joint-stock companies.

Petty Bourgeois Socialism

The feudal aristocracy was not the only class that was ruined by the bourgeoisie, not the only class whose conditions of existence pined and perished in the atmosphere of modern bourgeois society. The medieval burgesses and the small peasant bourgeoisie, were the precursors of the modern bourgeoisie. In those countries which are but little developed, industrially and commercially, these two classes still vegetate side by side with the rising bourgeoisie.

In countries where modern civilization has become fully developed, a new class of petty bourgeois has been formed, fluctuating between proletariat and bourgeoisie, and ever renewing itself as a supplementary part of bourgeoisie society. The individual members, of this class, however, are being constantly hurled down into the proletariat by the action of competition, and, as modern industry develops, they can see the moment approaching when they will completely disappear as an independent section of modern society, to be replaced, in manufacture, agriculture and commerce, by over-lookers, bailiffs and shop-men.

In countries like France, where the peasants constitute far more than half of the population, it was natural that writers who sided with the proletariat against the bourgeoisie, should use, in their criticism of the bourgeoisie regime, the standard of the peasant and petty bourgeois, and from the standpoint of these intermediate classes should take up the cudgels for the working class. Thus arose petty bourgeois Socialism. Sismondi was the head of this school, not only in France, but also in England.

This school of Socialism dissected with great acuteness the contradictions in the conditions of modern production. It laid bare the hypocritical apologies of economists. It proved, incontrovertibly, the disastrous effects of machinery and division of labor; the concentration of capital and land in a few hands; overproduction and crises; it pointed out the inevitable ruin of the petty bourgeois and peasant, the misery of the proletariat, the anarchy in production, the crying inequalities in the distribution of wealth, the industrial war of extermination between nations, the dissolution of old moral bonds, of the old family relations, of the old nationalities.

In its positive aims, however, this form of Socialism aspires either to restoring the old means of production and of exchange, and with them the old property relations, and the old society, or to cramping the modern means of production and of exchange, within the framework of the old property relations that have been, and were bound to be exploded by those means. In either case, it is both reactionary and Utopian.

Its last words are: corporate guilds for manufacture; patriarchal relations in agriculture.

Ultimately, when stubborn historical facts had dispersed all intoxicating effects of self-deception, this form of Socialism ended in a miserable fit of the blues.

German or "True" Socialism

The Socialist and Communist literature of France, a literature that originated under the pressure of a bourgeoisie in power, and that was the expression of the struggle against this power, was introduced into Germany at a time when the bourgeoisie, in that country, had just begun its contest with feudal absolutism.

German philosophers, would-be philosophers, and beaux esprits, eagerly seized on this literature, only forgetting, that when these writings immigrated from France into Germany, French social conditions had not immigrated along with them. In contact with German social conditions, this French literature lost all its immediate practical significance and assumed a purely literary aspect. Thus, to the German philosophers of the Eighteenth Century, the demands of the first French Revolution were nothing more than the demands of "Practical Reason" in general, and the utterance of the will of the revolutionary French bourgeoisie signified in their eyes the laws of pure Will, of Will as it was bound to be, of true human Will generally.

The work of the German literati consisted solely in bringing the new French ideas into harmony with their ancient philosophical

conscience, or rather, in annexing the French
ideas without deserting their own philosophical point of view.

This annexation took place in the same way
in which a foreign language is appropriated,
namely by translation.

It is well known how the monks wrote silly
lives of Catholic Saints over the manuscripts
on which the classical works of ancient hea-
thendom had been written. The German literati reversed this process with the profane
French literature. They wrote their philosophical nonsense beneath the French original. For instance, beneath the French criticism of the economic functions of money,
they wrote "Alienation of Humanity," and beneath the French criticism of the bourgeois
State they wrote, "Dethronement of the Category of the General," and so forth.

The introduction of these philosophical
phrases at the back of the French historical
criticisms they dubbed "Philosophy of Action," "True Socialism," "German Science of
Socialism," "Philosophical Foundation of Socialism," and so on.

The French Socialist and Communist literature was thus completely emasculated. And,

since it ceased in the hands of the German to express the struggle of one class with the other, he felt conscious of having overcome "French one-sidedness" and of representing, not true requirements, but the requirements of Truth, not the interests of the proletariat, but the interests of Human Nature, of Man in general, who belongs to no class, has no reality, who exists only in the misty realm of philosophical phantasy.

This German Socialism, which took its school-boy task so seriously and solemnly, and extolled its poor stock-in-trade in such mountebank fashion, meanwhile gradually lost its pedantic innocence.

The fight of the German, and especially, of the Prussian bourgeoisie, against feudal aristocracy and absolute monarchy, in other words, the liberal movement, became more earnest.

By this, the long-wished-for opportunity was offered to "True Socialism" of confronting the political movement with the socialist demands, of hurling the traditional anathemas against liberalism, against representative government, against bourgeois competition, bourgeois freedom of the press, bourgeois legislation, bourgeois liberty and equality, and of preaching to the masses that they had nothing to gain, and everything to lose, by this bourgeois movement. German Socialism forgot, in the nick of time, that the French criticism, whose silly echo it was, presupposed the existence of modern bourgeois society, with its corresponding economic conditions, and the political constitution adapted thereto, the very things whose attainment was the object of the pending struggle in Germany.

To the absolute governments, with their following of parsons, professors, country squires and officials, it served as a welcome scarecrow against the threatening bourgeoisie.

It was a sweet finish after the bitter pills of floggings and bullets, with which these same governments, just at that time, dosed the German working-class risings.

While this "True" Socialism thus served the government as a weapon for fighting the German bourgeoisie, it, at the same time, directly represented a reactionary interest, the interest of the German Philistines. In Germany the petty bourgeois class, a relic of the 16th century, and since then constantly cropping up again under various forms, is the real social basis of the existing state of things.

To preserve this class, is to preserve the existing state of things in Germany. The industrial and political supremacy of the bourgeoisie threatens it with certain destruction; on the one hand, from the concentration of capital; on the other, from the rise of a revolutionary proletariat. "True" Socialism appeared to kill these two birds with one stone. It spread like an epidemic.

The robe of speculative cobwebs, embroidered with flowers of rhetoric, steeped in the dew of sickly sentiment, this transcendental robe in which the German Socialists wrapped their sorry "eternal truths," all skin and bone, served to wonderfully increase the sale of their goods amongst such a public.

And on its part, German Socialism recognized, more and more, its own calling as the bombastic representative of the petty bourgeois Philistine.

It proclaimed the German nation to be the model nation, and the German petty Philistine to be the typical man. To every villainous meanness of this model man it gave a hidden, higher socialistic interpretation, the exact contrary of its true character. It went to the extreme length of directly opposing the "brutally destructive" tendency of Communism, and of proclaiming its supreme and impartial contempt of all class struggles. With very few exceptions, all the so-called Socialist and Communist publications that now (1847) circulate in Germany belong to the domain of this foul and enervating literature.

Conservative or Bourgeois Socialism

A part of the bourgeoisie is desirous of redressing social grievances, in order to secure the continued existence of bourgeois society.

To this section belong economists, philanthropists, humanitarians, improvers of the condition of the working class, organizers of charity, members of societies for the prevention of cruelty to animals, temperance fanatics, hole and corner reformers of every imaginable kind. This form of Socialism has, moreover, been worked out into complete systems.

We may cite Proudhon's "Philosophie de la Misere" as an example of this form.

The socialistic bourgeois want all the advantages of modern social conditions without the struggles and dangers necessarily resulting therefrom. They desire the existing state of society minus its revolutionary and disintegrating elements. They wish for a bourgeoisie without a proletariat. The bourgeoisie naturally conceives the world in which it is supreme to be the best; and bourgeois socialism develops this comfortable conception into various more or less complete systems. In requiring the proletariat to carry out such a system, and thereby to march straightway into the social New Jerusalem, it but requires in reality, that the proletariat should remain within the bounds of existing society, but should cast away all its hateful ideas concerning the bourgeoisie.

A second and more practical, but less systematic, form of this socialism sought to depreciate every revolutionary movement in the eyes of the working class, by showing that no mere political reform, but only a change in the material conditions of existence, in economical relations, could be of any advantage to them. By changes in the material conditions of existence, this form of Socialism, however, by no means understands abolition of the bourgeois relations of production, an abolition that can be effected only by a revolution, but administrative reforms, based on the continued existence of these relations; reforms, therefore, that in no respect affect the relations between capital and labor, but, at the best, lessen the cost, and simplify the administrative work, of bourgeois government.

Bourgeois Socialism attains adequate expression, when, and only when, it becomes a mere figure of speech.

Free trade: for the benefit of the working class. Protective duties: for the benefit of the working class. Prison Reform: for the benefit of the working class. This is the last word and the only seriously meant word of bourgeois Socialism.

It is summed up in the phrase: the bourgeois is a bourgeois—for the benefit of the working class.

Critical-Utopian Socialism and Communism

We do not here refer to that literature which, in every great modern revolution, has always given voice to the demands of the proletariat: such as the writings of Babeuf and others.

The first direct attempts of the proletariat to attain its own ends were made in times of universal excitement, when feudal society was being overthrown. These attempts necessarily failed, owing to the then undeveloped state of the proletariat, as well as to the absence of the economic conditions for its emancipation, conditions that had yet to be produced by the impending bourgeois epoch alone. The revolutionary literature that accompanied these first movements of the proletariat had necessarily a reactionary character. It inculcated universal asceticism and social leveling in its crudest form.

The Socialist and Communist systems properly so-called, those of St. Simon, Fourier, Owen and others, springs into existence in the early undeveloped period, described above, of the struggle between proletariat and bourgeoisie (see section I, Bourgeois and Proletarians).

The founders of these systems see, indeed, the class antagonisms, as well as the action of the decomposing elements in the prevailing form of society. But the proletariat, as yet in its infancy, offers to them the spectacle of a class without any historical initiative or any independent political movement.

Since the development of class antagonism keeps even pace with the development of industry, the economic situation, as they find it, does not as yet offer to them the material conditions for the emancipation of the proletariat. They therefore search after a new social science, after new social laws, that are to create these conditions.

Historical action is to yield to their personal inventive action, historically created conditions of emancipation to fantastic ones, and the gradual, spontaneous class-organization of the proletariat to an organization of society specially contrived by these inventors. Future history resolves itself, in their eyes, into the propaganda and the practical carrying out of their social plans.

In the formation of their plans they are conscious of caring chiefly for the interests of the working-class, as being the most suffering class. Only from the point of view of being the most suffering class does the proletariat exist for them.

The undeveloped state of the class struggle, as well as their own surroundings, cause Socialists of this kind to consider themselves far superior to all class antagonisms. They want to improve the condition of every member of society, even that of the most favored. Hence they habitually appeal to society at large, without distinction of class; nay, by preference, to the ruling class. For how can people, when once they understand their system, fail to see in it the best possible plan of the best posible state of society?

Hence, they reject all political, and especially all revolutionary action; they wish to attain their ends by peaceful means, and endeavor, by small experiments, necessarily doomed to failure, and by the force of example, to pave the way for the new social Gospel.

Such fantastic pictures of future society, painted at a time when the proletariat is still in a very undeveloped state, and has but a fantastic conception of its own position, correspond with the first instinctive yearnings of that class for a general reconstruction of society.

But these Socialist and Communist publi-

cations contain a critical element. They attack
every principle of existing society. Hence they
are full of the most valuable materials for the
enlightenment of the working class. The practical measures proposed in them, such as the
abolition of the distinction between town and
country, of the family, of the carrying on of
industries for the account of private individ-
uals, and of the wage system, the proclama-
tion of social harmony, the conversion of the
functions of the State into a mere superin-
tendence of production, all these proposals
point solely to the disappearance of class-
antagonisms which were, at that time, only
just cropping up, and which, in these publications, are recognized under their earliest,
indistinct and undefined forms only. These
proposals, therefore, are of a purely Utopian
character.

The significance of Critical-Utopian Socialism and Communism bears an inverse
relation to historical development. In proportion as the modern class struggle develops
and takes definite shape, this fantastic stand-
ing apart from the contest, these fantastic
attacks on it lose all practical value and all
theoretical justification. Therefore, although

the originators of these systems were, in many respects, revolutionary, their disciples have, in every case, formed mere reactionary sects. They hold fast by the original views of their masters, in opposition to the progressive historical development of the proletariat. They therefore endeavor, and that consistently, to deaden the class struggle and to reconcile the class antagonisms. They still dream of experimental relations of their social Utopias, of founding isolated "phalansteres," of establishing "Home Colonies," of setting up a "Little Icaria"[3]—duodecimo editions of the New Jerusalem, and to realize all these castles in the air, they are compelled to appeal to the feelings and purses of the bourgeois. By degrees they sink into the category of the reactionary conservative Socialists depicted above, differing from these only by more systematic pedantry, and by their fanatical and superstitious belief in the miraculous effects of their social science.

They, therefore, violently, oppose all po-

3. Phalansteres were socialist colonies on the plan of Charles Fourier. Icaria was the name given by Cabot to his Utopia and, later on, to his American Communist colony.

litical action on the part of the working class; such action, according to them, can only result from blind unbelief in the new Gospel.

The Owenites in England, and the Fourierists in France, respectively, opposed the Chartists and the "Reformists."

IV

Position of the Communists in Relation to the Various Existing Opposition Parties

Section II has made clear the relations of the Communists to the existing working-class parties, such as the Chartists in England and the Agrarian Reformers in America.

The Communists fight for the attainment of the immediate aims, for the enforcement of the momentary interests of the working class; but in the movement of the present, they also represent and take care of the future of that movement. In France the Communists ally themselves with the Social-Democrats,[1]

1. The party then represented in parliament by Ledru-Rollin, in literature by Louis Blanc, in the daily press by the Reform. The name of Social Democracy signified, with these its inventors, a section of the Democratic or Republican party more or less tinged with Socialism.

against the conservatives and radical bourgeoisie, reserving, however, the rights to take up a critical position in regard to phrases and illusions traditionally handed down from the great Revolution.

In Switzerland they support the Radicals, without losing sight of the fact that this party consists of antagonistic elements, partly of Democratic Socialists, in the French sense, partly of radical bourgeois.

In Poland they support the party that insists on an agrarian revolution, as the prime condition for national emancipation, that party which fomented the insurrection of Cracow in 1846.

In Germany they fight with the bourgeoisie whenever it acts in a revolutionary way, against the absolute monarchy, the feudal squirearchy, and the petty bourgeoisie.

But they never cease, for a single instant, to instill into the working class the clearest possible recognition of the hostile antagonism between bourgeoisie and proletariat, in order that the German workers may straightway use, as so many weapons against the bourgeoisie, the social and political conditions that the bourgeoisie must necessarily introduce along with its supremacy, and in order that, after the fall of the reactionary classes in Germany, the fight against the bourgeoisie itself may immediately begin.

The Communists turn their attention chiefly to Germany, because that country is on the eve of a bourgeois revolution, that is bound to be carried out under more advanced conditions of European civilization, and with a more developed proletariat, than that of England was in the seventeenth, and of France in the eighteenth century, and because the bourgeois revolution in Germany will be but the prelude to an immediately following proletarian revolution.

In short, the Communists everywhere support every revolutionary movement against the existing social and political order of things.

In all these movements they bring to the front, as the leading question in each, the property question, no matter what its degree of development at the time.

Finally, they labor everywhere for the union and agreement of the democratic parties of all countries.

The Communists disdain to conceal their

views and aims. They openly declare that their ends can be attained only by the forcible overthrow of all existing social conditions. Let the ruling classes tremble at a Communist revolution. The proletarians have nothing to lose but their chains. They have a world to win.

Working men of all countries, unite!